The minds of violent people

An insight into how the violent mind works

Natasha Ray.

Table of contents

Chapter 1

Understanding violence and looking at its causes

Millions of people worldwide are killed by violence every year, making it one of the main causes of mortality around the globe.
While violence exists in every nation, the bulk of its fatalities takes place in low- to middle-income nations, many of which are experiencing internal strife. Although more than half of violent killings take place outside of armed conflicts, it should be remembered that such deaths cannot only be ascribed to war.
Particularly in metropolitan areas, violence has grown more interpersonal and associated with criminal activities. Intentional homicide accounts for about half of all fatalities worldwide.

It's also crucial to remember that violence, which also leads to non-fatal, sexual, and psychological abuse, is a major contributor to the health and societal cost that may be ascribed to it. Violence also has a significant negative impact on community economies, social welfare agencies, and the legal and health systems.
Violence has negative impacts on a nation that affect not just its inhabitants but also the community and nation as a whole. Violence has a direct and considerable negative influence on economic development in many nations, which makes it difficult to eradicate poverty. In addition, violence leads to severe psychological and physical trauma, which lowers the quality of life for everyone in society.

Although violence is often seen and addressed as an unavoidable aspect of the human condition, such presumptions are changing, the scope of the discussion is expanding, and a greater emphasis is being put on the avoidance of violent behavior and its negative effects.
An improvement in our knowledge of this complicated phenomenon is necessary for the efficacy of preventative efforts. Although moral standards

may differ greatly across cultures, which makes it more difficult to discuss the very delicate subject of violence, its origins, and its effects, some kind of consensus must be achieved to properly defend human life and dignity.
Purposeful use of physical force or power, whether threatened or used, against oneself, another person, a group of people, or a community that causes or is very likely to cause damage, such as injury, death, psychological harm, maldevelopment, or deprivation.
Contrarily, violence is a kind of physical aggressiveness that almost always causes injury. Whether a violent act is regarded as a crime varies from nation to nation and may vary over time as nations modify their laws in response to shifting political systems and societal mores. To react effectively and implement effective preventative measures, it is crucial to comprehend the distinction between these two ideas.

Studies have linked suicide, severe displays of hostility against others, and violence.
overlap to some level, an excessive display of hostility aimed towards oneself. For a long time, researchers have worked to understand why some people behave aggressively against themselves while others vent their rage in public. Finding the negative thinking patterns that persons who are at high risk for violence or suicide encounter may hold the key to the solution.
Family and societal dynamics are strongly correlated with the pandemic of violence in our nation. Therefore, a focus on the child's early experiences, the parent-child relationship, parental characteristics, and child-rearing methods can help to shed light on how childhood trauma and the resulting shame are internalized in the form of hostile thoughts and attitudes toward others, which can eventually result in violent acts.

- Identification with the Aggressor: When children are the target of anger and violence, whether overt or covert, it's common for the aggressor to adopt the persona of the irrational, enraged parent. They incorporate their furious parenting styles, which results in the crucial dualism between the self and the anti-self systems in the psyche. The strategy of identifying with the aggressor may assist to reduce anxiety, but doing so forces the kid to absorb the parent's fury or anger, which the youngster may then express via aggressive, assaultive behaviors against other people. It is possible to think of violence as the reactivation or expression of this internalized hostility.

- Dissociation: People who had traumatic, abusive, or neglectful childhoods and who also suffered voice attacks tend to dissociate more often, more intensely, and with more damaging voice attacks than people who had less severe or non-abusive voice assaults. According to research, stress-related dissociation and poor brain functioning, such as seeing violence or experiencing physical child abuse, predispose adolescents and adults to aggressive or violent acting-out behavior.

Perspectives on the Violent Mind

We may escape having to comprehend the aggressive mentality by both glamorizing and denouncing violence. To provide therapy for violent individuals and to foresee the kind of hazards they pose to both themselves and society, we need to penetrate their subjective world.

My awareness of human destructiveness toward oneself and others has been deepened by clinical material that my colleagues and I have seen over the last forty years. A critical cognitive process that underlies all sorts of maladaptive behavior, I realized, is at its foundation. This critical thinking process, which I've come to refer to as the "voice," is an internalization of unpleasant events and attitudes toward the kid. People who experience this inner adversary become antagonistic toward themselves as well as scared, incensed, and distrustful of others.

I created a scale to gauge the risk of suicide after researching the voices connected to suicidal thoughts in the past. Items were founded on a sequence of self-criticism and self-attacks that became progressively worse. Customers were asked to recommend which products they used and how often. The measure successfully and significantly differentiates between suicidal and non-suicidal people. We used the same reasoning to comprehend and anticipate violence and created a scale made up of furious, hostile sentiments relative to others. Our study was successful in outlining the factors that contribute to aggression and violent behavior.

Evaluation of the Risk of Violence

It is essential to pinpoint the precise cognitive processes that control violent behavioral reactions to accurately predict the likelihood of violence in high-risk people. Violence is also greatly influenced by overtly hostile voices. These speakers openly call for using violence. They persuade someone that engaging in aggressive and violent behavior would be acceptable, or that doing so would be a welcome relief, or even enjoyable. The individual who is persuaded by these voices does not express any regret. These voices may be heard saying things like, "Violence is the answer." You'll feel better if you just crush them. By

There is a strong correlation between five degrees of damaging thought and violent behavior:

The voices at Level 1 were classified as "Paranoid/Suspicious" and said things like "You can only trust your kind." Alternatively, everyone is keeping something from you. Alternatively, keep the immigrants outside—they don't deserve anything. or Never put your faith in a woman (man).

The second level, dubbed "Persecuted Misfit," had voices saying things like "They don't give a damn about you." Or maybe they're simply trying to offend you. Or your contributions go unnoticed. Nobody thinks highly of you. Alternatively, he (she) could be exploiting you.

"Self-deprecating/Pseudo-independent" was the description of Level 3, which had voices that said things like ``You're truly in danger now. You have no credibility. Or you should take care of yourself. No other will. or You constantly caused issues. You are constantly to blame.

Level 4 was categorized as "Overt Aggressive" and included sounds that threatened to smash the offender if they didn't listen. You'll let them know who's in charge! Do you not like the way that gun feels in your hand?

Level 5, included voices like You're a remarkable person. or Anything is possible if you set your mind to it. Or You're a Powerhouse. It's interesting to note that many instances of both domestic and criminal violence have been linked to narcissistic rage that is sparked by situations that are perceived as endangering the perpetrator's vanity or inflated self-esteem.

Understanding violence requires revealing what is happening in the violent person's mind as well as verbalizing the destructive thoughts that motivate acts of criminal and interpersonal violence. The level of violent behavior will depend on how much internalized, hostile voices intensify or escalate. It is possible to stop negative thoughts from turning into harmful deeds by becoming aware of the development of cynical, critical voices toward others and recognizing them as a warning sign.

The majority of the violence in our society is, according to research, committed by a relatively small group of persistent repeat offenders. The majority of these people could receive treatment in a setting that is therapeutically appropriate, sparing them and future victims' suffering.
The effects of cruelty and violence, whether they occur inside families or across countries, are a major issue because they undermine all other attempts to create communities that are balanced, fair, and compassionate. The biological, physiological, and psychosocial aspects of violence, aggression, and trauma have been the subject of countless scientific and clinical studies.

Violence is known to be caused by a variety of factors, such as abusive parenting, temperamental and genetic susceptibility, mood disorders, medical imitators, and dual disorders, as well as the aftereffects of trauma, abuse and neglect, brain injury, drug abuse, peer pressure, and media overload. Violence is a generational issue. An abusive parent is more likely to have experienced abuse as a kid. A mother who has been beaten is more likely to maltreat or neglect her kid. According to studies, jailed and homeless women encounter substantial rates of prior abuse.

Antisocial conduct may be avoided or treated for a variety of situations. A person who acts violently, aggressively, or sadistically is likely to have severe neurochemical or hormonal imbalances as a result of brain traumas, epilepsy and mood disorders, or drug misuse. Brain activity scans often reveal signs of these abnormalities, which may be treated.

For instance, parents who are unprepared or unsupported are more likely to connect inappropriately with their newborns or young children, which might result in attachment issues, which are related to subsequent antisocial behavior. Learning difficulties are associated with inadequate prenatal care, malnutrition, and exposure to toxins; if undiagnosed and untreated, these can result in behavioral or academic issues.

There has been evidence for some time that child traumatization has devastating effects on society, but we are still not allowed to acknowledge this reality. This information affects every one of us and, if widely shared, should bring about fundamental social change, most importantly a halt to the violence's unchecked rise. I want to emphasize the following points to make my point clearer:

Every child is born with the capacity to learn, advance, live, fall in love, and express their needs and emotions to defend themselves.

Children require the respect and care of adults who value them, care about them, and genuinely assist them in developing a sense of self and identity for their growth.

Children's integrity will be permanently damaged if these fundamental requirements are not met and instead, they are mistreated to satisfy the demands of adults by being taken advantage of, abused, punished, manipulated, ignored, or fooled without any outside help.

Anger and pain are the expected responses to such harm. However, as children in this abusive environment are not allowed to vent their rage and since it would be intolerable for them to feel their suffering alone, they are forced to repress their emotions, erase all memories of the trauma, and idealize those who perpetrated the abuse. They won't remember what happened to them later on.

Their feelings of rage, helplessness, despair, longing, anxiety, and pain, which are dissociated from the original cause, will manifest in destructive acts toward other people (criminal behavior, mass murder) or toward themselves (drug addiction, alcoholism, prostitution, psychic disorders, suicide).

When these individuals have children, they frequently use them as scapegoats in their acts of retaliation for being mistreated as children. As long as it is considered to be a necessary part of raising children, child abuse is still tolerated in our society and is even regarded favorably. Tragically, parents beat their kids to get away from the feelings brought on by how their parents treated them.

Mistreated youngsters must at least once in their lives come into touch with someone certain that the environment, not the defenseless, abused kid, is to blame if they are to avoid becoming criminals or mentally sick. In this way, society's knowledge or ignorance may play a crucial role in either preserving or destroying a life. Herein lies the fantastic chance for loved ones, social workers, therapists, educators, medical professionals, psychiatric staff, and nurses to support and believe the kid.

Society has up to now shielded the adult and placed the guilt on the victim. Theories that still adhere to the educational concepts of our great-grandparents, according to which children are seen as clever beings, ruled by malevolent urges, who fabricate tales and attack their innocent parents or seek them sexually, have assisted in this blindness. In actuality, kids prefer to take the blame for their parents' mistreatment on themselves and exonerate their usually loving parents.

Through innovative therapy techniques, it has been shown for some time that repressed traumatic memories from childhood remain retained in the body and, albeit unconscious, continue to have an impact far into adulthood. Additionally, electronic fetal testing has shown something that most adults were previously unaware of: a kid reacts to and picks up on both kindness and cruelty from an early age.

Once the painful events of childhood are no longer required to stay concealed in the dark, even the most ludicrous conduct exposes its previously hidden rationale in the light of this new understanding.
The propagation of violence from generation to generation will naturally come to a stop as a result of our increased awareness of the cruelty with which children are treated, which was previously often ignored, as well as the effects of such treatment.
People whose integrity has not been compromised throughout childhood will be clever, receptive, empathetic, and extremely sensitive both in their youth and in maturity. These people were also safeguarded, respected, and treated with honesty by their parents. They will enjoy life and not feel the urge to harm themselves or others, much alone murder them. Instead of attacking others, they will use their strength to protect themselves. Because of what they have learned from their own experience and because this knowledge (and not the experience of cruelty) has been ingrained in them since the beginning, they will be unable to do anything other than respect and protect those who are weaker than themselves, including their children. Such individuals would find it incomprehensible that prior generations had to develop a massive war industry to feel secure and at home in this environment. They will be able to respond to intimidation tactics in their adult lives more logically and creatively since it won't be their unconscious impulse to avoid intimidation encountered from a very young age.

Chapter 2

Knowledge of the violent mind

Violence, just like every other activity, starts in the brain. It begins with a series of perspectives that is at the end carried on. It's typically stimulated by gloomy feelings, for example, fear, anger, sadness, and disappointment as talked about earlier. Understanding what is happening in the brain of somebody who is fierce permits us to all the more likely evaluate the gamble for savagery and to mediate, safeguarding both the possible culprit and casualty. Many gamble factors for brutality can't be changed, however, an individual's reasoning is a gamble factor that can be. By checking the decline in an individual's savage contemplations during treatment, we can evaluate their improvement. Besides, in offering brutal individuals comprehension of the considerations that underlie their tormented reasoning, we are giving them a method by which to wage war against the voices that draw them into demonstrations of viciousness.

We have seen that when we are areas of strength for encountering feelings joined by excitement, for example, when we are disappointed, furious, awkward, or restless about our demise, we might be bound to aggress. Notwithstanding, assuming that we know that we are feeling these gloomy feelings, we could attempt to find an answer to keeping ourselves from attacking others. Maybe, we could suppose, on the off chance that we can deliver our pessimistic feelings in a somewhat innocuous manner, then, at that point, the likelihood that we will be aggressive could diminish. Perhaps you have attempted this strategy. Have you at any point attempted to holler truly clearly, hit a pad, or kick something when you are irate, with the expectation that doing so will deliver your forceful propensities?

Both glamorizing and disparaging viciousness assist us in trying not to need to grasp the savage psyche. We ought to enter the brutal individual's emotional world, not simply to have the option to offer treatment, yet in addition, to expect the idea of the dangers, they encapsulate both to themselves and society.

Towards a Formative indication of hostility coordinated against oneself, cross-over somewhat. Specialists have long endeavored to all the more likely comprehend the reason why a few people carry on hostility toward themselves while others express their displeasure. A piece of the response seems to lie in distinguishing the negative manners of thinking experienced by the people who are at a high gamble for one or the other self-destruction or brutality.

We have become mindful of a basic decisive point of view that is at the center of all types of maladaptive ways of behaving. I named this decisive manner of thinking the "voice." It addresses the assimilation of difficult encounters and negative mentalities that were coordinated toward the kid. This adversary inside makes individuals feel antagonistic toward themselves and unfortunate, furious, and dubious toward others.

Basic Inward Voices Fundamental Vicious Way of behaving

The basic internal voice upholds a singular's negative personality, prompting both self-assault and aggression toward others. This assisted me with recognizing a split in the character between the self framework and the counter-self framework. The division of the psyche mirrors an essential split between powers that address oneself and those that go against or endeavor to obliterate it.

Damaging activities coordinated against others happen when sensations of dissatisfaction are joined with negative mental cycles. Since individuals channel occasions through voice interaction, during seasons of pressure even harmless episodes can be pervaded with a negative stacking.

Certain individuals will quite often mutilate others or view them with doubt, bringing about an essential distrustful or exploited direction toward life. Their voices grant negative data to them about others: He's simply exploiting you. Or then again, She's continuously interfering in your life. Outrageous negative voices are at the center of all types of criminal and abusive behavior at home and hazardous ways of behaving.

People who carry on rough motivations legitimize their activities as being legitimately merited by their casualties. A method of reasoning that supports vindictive activity is likewise characteristic of culprits of aggressive behavior at home: She made them come to her. She realized which buttons to push to make me detonate. Or on the other hand, I'll settle the score with that knave. Perhaps in the future, he'll reconsider playing with me.

A neurotic direction comes from the projection of one's gloomy feelings and voices onto others. At the point when individuals dread their resentment, they will generally abandon it by extending it to others. Then they see them as undermining and perilous, will generally carry on prudently against others, and frequently incite the very animosity or harmful treatment they dread. The outcome is an unavoidable outcome and a spiraling impact that can finish in a heightening of the forceful way of behaving or brutality.
Time after time, the subject of savagery is tended to in our general public from a foundation of emotionalism, nausea, and fear. The revealing of savage occasions induces two responses from watchers: sickened interest or a repulsed reflex to dismiss. Neither one of the responses slants us to look for a superior comprehension of why viciousness happens, nor to pose the inquiry: What makes a person brutal?

The media's weighted spotlight on the impacts of brutality rather than the causes isn't altogether to blame for our protection from investigating the underlying foundations of savagery. Some portion of our reluctance comes from the way that brutality is a profoundly upsetting issue. A brutal way of behaving can be set off by disappointment, outrage, or an apparent embarrassment. Its motivation can be to fight back, threaten, or apply control. It is just when we have a superior comprehension of viciousness that we can start to have an effect.

Even though there isn't one response to what causes viciousness, there is something that has offered significant knowledge into what happens in the brain of somebody who is rough. They are classified as "voices" (negative perspectives) that flood the personalities of these people impacting them to participate in demonstrations of savagery.

These "voices" aren't capable of mental trips yet rather are a methodical example of negative contemplations against oneself and unfriendly and dubious toward others. We refer to these damaging contemplations as "voices" because a large number of individuals we talked with detailed encountering them that way.

This chapter isn't just useful for anticipating rough aim yet in addition to giving a general comprehension that makes sense of a wide range of viciousness from the outrageous models that stand out as truly newsworthy to the furious and brutal responses that we sense in ourselves as well as other people.

The possibility that taking part in less hurtful forceful activities will diminish the propensity to aggress later in a more destructive manner, known as therapy, is an old one. It was referenced as a way.

The facts confirm that decreasing adverse consequences and excitement can lessen the probability of hostility. For example, assuming we can occupy ourselves from our gloomy feelings or our dissatisfaction by accomplishing something different, instead of ruminating on it, we can feel significantly improved and will be less inclined to aggress. In any case, to the extent that social analysts have had the option to decide, endeavoring to eliminate gloomy feelings by participating in or noticing forceful ways of behaving (that is, the possibility of therapy) just doesn't work.

On the off chance that an individual appreciates taking part in the forceful way of behaving, they might be compensated, making them bound to take part in it once more. Also, hostility helps us to remember the chance of being forceful in light of our dissatisfactions. In aggregate, depending on therapy by taking part in or seeing hostility is a perilous way of behaving — it is bound to build the blazes of animosity rather than to put them out. It is smarter to just allow the disappointment to disseminate over the long run or maybe to take part in other peaceful however diverting exercises.

Nervousness can be a mistaking condition for the individuals who experience it and can be much more confounding for the people who have not and by experienced it. Many individuals without a background marked by nervousness botch tension for dread however uneasiness isn't necessarily dread. Tension is just a dreaded reaction yet may not be in light of dread-related triggers. Nervousness itself additionally has many different side effects that can be confounding, disturbing, and upsetting.

Fierce considerations are an illustration of a distressing side effect, the individuals who experience this side effect might find it consoling to realize that this is certainly not an extraordinary side effect. Brutal considerations themselves may not seem like nervousness, but rather they can be straightforwardly connected with explicit uneasiness issues.
Do you have vicious contemplations you have no control over? A few kinds of nervousness cause thought concealment, which makes considerations return more grounded than previously.

Vicious Considerations Are Ordinary Contemplations Gone Wild
The principal thing to acknowledge is that rough contemplations don't begin as a nervousness side effect, nor do they matter about your character. They're contemplations - the very kinds of considerations that a great many people have and neglect. Tension is just a purpose that brings them out more.
Brutal considerations are generally normal in those with a fanatical impulsive problem, even though they might influence any sort of nervousness.

Grasping the Reason for Brutal Considerations
At the point when we discuss these contemplations, we're discussing any figure that one should seriously think about as vicious.
These may not appear as though they're brought about by uneasiness because in a way they're not. But on the other hand, they're not strange for those encountering uneasiness. Many individuals have irregular blazes of these kinds of contemplations that they neglect so rapidly that they don't for even a moment acknowledge they have them. Minds are only that - minds. At times an individual fantasizes and pictures something rough. It works out, and the vast majority fail to remember it.

The issue is that those with tension never appear to fail to remember it. Those with uneasiness will generally ponder them again and again. Intriguing that the fundamental explanation for this happens is that you're attempting to fail to remember it.

Interrupt and answer these ten inquiries as yes or no genuinely;
1)When somebody speaks harshly to me, I use whatever might remain of the day mulling over everything.
2)I have hot as well as cold bursts.
3)I trepidation swarms, being let be, the dull, outcasts, or traffic.
4)I don't rest easier thinking about myself
5)I have sweat-splashed or cold, moist hands
6)I will as a general rule base on upsetting conditions or events happening in my life.
7)I am always upset.
8)To me, the world is a startling spot
9)I feel I'm letting go.
10)I experience jolting, shivering, or feeble opinions.

Expecting yes is your answer for past what a major piece of these requests that could be a pointer that you have been having horrendous considerations and you could have unpleasant penchants.
This test is certainly not 100% sure, in any case, it's an inclination.
To know and understand the characters of severe people we need to grasp the thoughts that go before egregious demonstrations. A piece of those contemplations that have been kept in the past segment will be analyzed under:

- Paranoia/wary thoughts: These hypochondriacs and questionable contemplations encourage people to anticipate a self-cautious and safeguarded act from an obvious gamble. Since the anxiety and misperception passes the terrorizing show up to be certifiable, people figure out upheld in acting viciousness to shield themselves. The incredulity is maintained by negative voices about others being extraordinary, surprising, and dreadful.

These voices add to a singular's uncertainty and the question of the world at large.

A delineation of such voices is: They are determined to get you. "Have almost no confidence in them".

A person with this kind of thought will continually answer problematically around those people who seem "not to like him" which finally could incite savage emissions. These sorts of individuals will see everything said or made as showing harm to them. Anyone he meets is a conceivably hazardous individual, at whatever point he has cured, a watchfulness rings to him to answer brutally.

- Deprecating contemplations: Various voices that lead to brutality are the ones that help people feel misdirected and persecuted. They urge a person that he/she is the overcomer of maltreatment by others. These voices advance and sponsor contemplations of being restricted, denounced, or humiliated by others. An outline of these voices is: They will humiliate you. "They don't seriously see you". A person with low certainty will presumably think this way or someone who has been consistently put down, or embarrassed in public. He feels he is the vital person who maintains himself. No other person minds, subsequently wanting to monitor himself from"potential cynics".

- Self-decaying thoughts: Violent people have furthermore nitty gritty self-degrading voices that make them feel that they are disgusting and that no one will appreciate or regularly ponder them. These voices advance isolation and the inclination of a person to manage him/herself. They attack others and view them as excusing. These voices invigorate an individual not requiring anything from some other individual. An outline of these voices is: "you ought to manage yourself" considering the way that no one else will. Don't expect anything from anyone, you might be baffled.Presumptuous examinations: these voices can be a herald of viciousness too because they advance a view that an individual is superior to other people and ought to be dealt with subsequently. They support an extended mental self-representation that capacities to compensate for solidly settled self-hatred. Exactly when the celebrated character is sabotaged, for example by attacks or sore ignored, an individual often answers savagely with an ultimate objective to recuperate the amplified mental self-representation. Research that joins high trust in young people to violence truly assessed extended certainty or vanity. A representation of these voices is: You are a particularly incredible arrangement better contrasted with them. How should they dare to talk with you like that!!. These can happen when people have been acclimated with having their heading or having anything they want when they were kids. As of now as adults they expect they save the choice to everything including what has a spot with others. They accept they are a particularly incredible arrangement better contrasted with everyone.

Chapter 3

The best methodology is to take the necessary steps not to be seriously abused.

Seeing a picture of an extreme grown-up, it's trying to envision the guiltless youngster they used to be. Is there such an amazing concept as being envisioned as a savage? Are there, for sure, "terrible seeds" concerning human existence? Like such endless traits, seriousness consolidates a genuine relationship between inborn qualities and climate. We can not change the DNA we are brought into the world with, yet we can strongly influence how these attributes are bestowed. With each of the elements shown to add to violence risk, we can at no point, later on, say that crazy people are simply "thought about like that." There is a ton we can do to forestall seriousness, and barely anybody at any stage in life is miserable or irredeemable.

Seriousness is the result of a mix of ordinary, social, and mental parts, particularly those that increment openness to inadequacy, disgrace, and embarrassment. Forestalling antagonism should consolidate the converse: engaging sure individuals, much of the time contemplated, and related, while guaranteeing they have a sound and reasonable character regard, and certainty.

The individual who is being savage could try to cause you to feel cautious, embarrassed, or responsible about what's going on at home. You are not to fault for their activities - what they have done is off track. It isn't your shortcoming and it's beginning and end except for a stand-out confidential. Family brutality is an awful way of behaving.

Try not to accept them expecting that they will change. something repulsive may happen to you on the off chance that you enlighten somebody concerning what's going on at home. Certain individuals will tune in and can help you.

It is hazardous to Stay quiet about family violence. It's alright to tell somebody and it will help you and your family to turn out to be more protected.
Nothing is stunning such that it can't be discussed.Help is accessible.
Savagery isn't just physical yet can comparatively be a private or action word. While keeping away from a terrible individual, the following are a few, generally speaking, things to zero in on:

- Indications of a background marked by substance use/misuse/reliance
- Difficult situations/serious anxiety attacks
- Noncompliance with the school authority
- Unquestionably wild tattoos
- Doesn't show pressure for legitimate and individual results
- Downloads bomb-creation recipes or coordinated data on showings of mass ruthlessness from the Internet
- Has developed a hit once-over of foes or has drawn plans for the school
- Seems to require fitting empathy toward the victim(s)
- Is seen during understudy interviews as remaining mindful of conceded looks
- Is seen as having indications of tumult during the understudy interview: pacing, grinding crushing hands, and teeth
- Presently, I will bundle several other advice signs under confidential direct rules to zero in on:

Obsession

- Trusts self to be an overcomer of a specific person
- Terrible opinions and critical vibes of hatred
- An express object of need
- Seen shameful acts, embarrassments, excuse
- Thoughts of death or different occasions of ruthlessness
- Confined center - "sees no real way to get out"- select fixation
- Proclaimed shows of viciousness
- Generally savage figures

- Barbarous music and different media
- Weapons and annihilation

Thoughts

- Battling with an occasion where he/she was strangely treated or embarrassed
- Impression of being absurdly treated
- Persecutory strays in dreamland with self as a misfortune
- Shaky
- Gazes vacantly at nothing in particular, overall
- Demand dreams
- Affected gazes vacantly at nothing in particular that consolidate power, control, obliteration
- On an exceptionally essential level incapacitated viewpoints

Verbal Signs

- Brief and winding dangers
- Conveying a savage strategy
- Dreary collapse dangers or explanations
- Passes a wish on to kill, to be killed, or a wish to kick the bucket
- Undermines or gloats about passing a weapon on to school
- Compromising/bothering calls or messages
- Confers harshness, sadness, or misery
- Analyzing terrible ways to deal with acting or dreams
- Nonsensical revoltingness (relevantly inappropriate)
- Testing or compromising pronouncements
- Compromising or perhaps wild talk
- Ridiculing or terrible language
- Confers energies of being bothered by different understudies and staff
- Conveys critical respect for school shooters
- Has analyzed plans for disturbance, yet when tended to, says he/she was kidding

Behavioral or physical clues

- Check out for the person's will in general savage media, for example, dazzling exhibition movies and first-individual shooter games
- Savage clothing (cover fatigues, unforgiving message shirts)
- Subverts peers/more vigorous, young people
- Following/surveilling relegated people
- Obliteration of property
- Aggravating
- Overcomer of tormenting or driving; feels concerns are being excused
- Self-destructing real appearance and managing oneself
- Obligation regarding making and data interfacing with known or thought can't deal with social events
- Inappropriate presentations of sentiments, especially shock, sadness, or fury
- Disconnected and disposed of; rejects correspondence
- Signs or history of substance use/misuse/reliance
- Difficult situations/ridiculous psychological breakdowns
- Noncompliance with the school authority
- Undeniably horrendous tattoos
- Doesn't show pressure for authentic and individual outcomes
- Downloads bomb-creation recipes or point-by-point data on showings of mass fierceness from Web
- Has energized a hit synopsis of foes or has drawn plans for the school
- History of being bothered or spurred following quite far back to straightforward years
- History of passing a weapon on to school
- History of upsetting exercises
- Has been embraced antipsychotic or impetus drugs

1. Desire and Possessiveness. Ought to be with you tenaciously. Issues you for boggling consistently. Seeks after you and a critical piece of the time calls. Requests that partners test you.

2. Controlling Way to deal with acting. Reliably questions who you contribute your energy with, what you did/wore/said, where you went. Makes you request that endorsement do unequivocal things. Acts, as you don't, can use clever impulse. Masks controlling way to deal with acting by professing to be focused on your success.

3. Fast Responsibility. A half year or less before living independently or getting. Claims unexplainable love. Strain for the obligation. Says you are the one explicitly who can cause him to feel in a like manner.

4. Ridiculous Assumptions. Comments you so much that establishes you radiate a connection of being excellent. Over-praising. Surmises that you should be awesome. Says, "I'm all you want. You are all I want."

5. Withdrawal. Puts down everybody you know-partners are either unseemly, scandalous, or you are cheating with them-family is extravagantly controlling, doesn't esteem you, or you are exorbitantly subject to them. Won't allow you to utilize a vehicle or visit on the telephone. Makes it pursuing for you to go to work or school. Tries to wipe out your assets as a whole.

6. Inadequacies Others for Issues. On the off chance that there are issues with the customary plan, it is all around another person's lack. Expecting that anything cuts off being horrendous in the friendship, is all your shortcomings. Won't get a sense of obligation with his own way to deal with acting.

7. Imperfections Others for Sentiments. Tries to cause you in danger for how they feel. "You're making me furious." "You're harming me by not doing what I inquire." "I can't battle the compulsion to be maddened." Won't get a sense of satisfaction from my perspective.

8. Unbelievable responsiveness. Aggravated. Trusts generally that to be a particular assault. Searches for battles. Conclusively overemphasizes things. Unconventional. You can never sort out what will disturb him.

9. Inconsiderate or Terrible to Other people. Repulses creatures or kids brutally. Inhumane toward torment and sulking. Urges kids until they cry. Doesn't advance toward others with concession. Disdainful of others' viewpoints.

10. "Energetic" Use of Power During Sexual Turn of events. Little worry about whether or not you need sex, and uses scowling or shock to push you toward consistency. Hits sexual or ruining fun at you.

11. Loud attack of Any Sort.

12. Undaunted Sex Occupations. Recognizes ladies are mediocrely differentiated from men. Inappropriate to be an entire individual without a relationship.

13. Startling disposition changes-like they have two characters. Brief good, one second from now detonating. One second pleased, one second from now irredeemable.

14. Past Battering. You could hear the individual was hazardous to another person. They say it's counterfeit, or their ex was "insane," or it wasn't too appalling.

15. Dangers of Any Sort.

16. Breaking or Striking Articles. Breaks loved impacts. Beats a table with grasp hands. Tosses objects.

17. Any Power During a Contention. Pushes or controls you from leaving the room.

18. Doesn't Regard Your Property or Confirmation.

Chapter 4

Guidelines to deal handle hostility or savage abuse

There are huge things you should remember to accept that you or someone in your family is being mauled. These include:
The unpleasant person could endeavor to make you feel careful, humiliated, or at risk about what's happening at home. You are not to blame for their exercises - what they have done is misguided. It isn't your issue and it's everything except a novel secret. Family violence is bad behavior.
Make an effort not to believe them if they offer something horrible will happen to you accepting you illuminate someone concerning what's happening at home. Some people will tune in and can help you.
Keeping silent about family brutality is dangerous. It's okay to tell someone and it will help you and your family to end up being more secure.
Nothing is shocking to the point that it can't be talked about.

1)Tell someone. Expecting you are the individual being referred to or are a spectator to ruthlessness, tell someone. It will in general be anyone you trust, similar to a buddy, parent, educator, guide, kin/sister, or neighbor.
Seriously view all severity and abuse. Remember that numerous shows of brutality and abuse are unlawful.
2)Stand firm. Expecting you to witness any sort of viciousness or abuse, stand up, step in, or holler out that the liable party is the horrendous one, and the fierceness needs to stop.
3)Be an individual. Have an autonomous viewpoint. Make an effort not to follow the gathering and don't give up to peer pressure. Participate in no kind of ruthlessness or abuse considering the way that your partners are.
Recover the power. Liable gatherings act violently or destructively to get power. By not sharing, you eliminate the power from the miscreant and pass it to the individual being referred to.
Remember, putting others down doesn't raise you. There won't ever be a substantial defense to be harsh or savage towards anyone.

Wrong. the entire day. Mercilessness and abuse of any kind that happens at whatever point is misguided. That's all anyone needs to know.
4)Be a buddy. Help the person who is being mauled by inviting them to participate in school works out. This will eliminate the vibe of being far off from every other person.
5)Let the news out. Comfort the person who was hurt and get the news out about it that what happened was irrational or justified.
Stay cool. Take the necessary steps not to answer fierceness with shock. Shock can intensify what is happening, you are as of now experiencing a forceful way of behaving at home:

- Plan how you could get away from the house quickly expecting your associate becomes fierce. Endeavor to arrange yourself near a doorway where you can escape quickly.
- Set up a pack and guard it at some spot, really open, and hidden away from your accessory. Load it with pieces of clothing for yourself as well as your children, remedy reorders and information, critical papers, vehicle keys, photographs, money, and emergency phone numbers. Add much else you could expect if you want to avoid with regards to no place (see list underneath).
- Have the phone numbers for neighboring safe houses and resources saved in a safeguarded spot with the objective that you can get to them quickly.
- Teach neighbors about the abuse and ask whether they hear disturbances coming from your home, such as calling your home, stopping by, or calling an accepted untouchable, which could be a buddy or relative, then again, in case it is safeguarded to do in that capacity, the police.
- Talk with your children about how they can watch themselves as well.

Expecting that you are considering leaving a destructive accessory:
Recognize things that have worked in the past to safeguard you.
Consider what has happened beforehand and how the lowlife has acted. Perceive signs that show when the scoundrel could become horrendous

(e.g., direct: non-verbal correspondence, drug/alcohol use, etc; and event-driven: paydays, events, etc.).
Yet again recognize how you will answer if the severity starts. Is it safeguarded to call the police? Is there a phone in the house? Might you anytime resolve a sign with the children or neighbors to track down help?
Research approaches to having dangerous weapons (e.g., guns, hunting sharp edges, etc) killed from the house.
Plan a break course and practice it. Know where you can go and who you can call for help. Keep a summary of addresses and phone numbers where you can go in crisis and keep them in a safeguarded spot.
If possible, open a record or hide money to spread out or increase opportunity.
If you are experiencing a forceful way of behaving at home:

Level one
Tracking down help
Contact an affiliation that can help. Most locales have close resources to help setbacks from abuse. If you don't have the foggiest idea where to start then again chat with someone about needing to leave a severe relationship

Level two
Find a Protected house that will help you.
If you are a woman who is at a loss from abuse, find a battered women's protected house in your space (or a nearby town). Realize that the genuine area of such sanctuaries is normally kept secret for the security of the women in the protected house, but you should have the choice to call a hotline or go through an isolating real region. Then, you will be insinuated in the protected house.

Most safe houses think about a safeguarded spot to reside for the two women and children. They are planned to offer prosperity and support while you monetarily recuperate, but your visit there will be for a confined proportion of the time.

Level three

Speak with Family or Colleagues

Unfortunately, various overcomers of abuse pull out or are constrained to become isolated. This often convinces setbacks to imagine that they have no one to help them with moving away from their miscreant. In any case, friends and family, whether or not you have been far off, may get past and help you with getting away from what is happening. Interface with someone you trust and solicit help.

Endeavor to be unequivocal with what you would like for them to achieve for you, (for instance, let you stay with them, keep your "move away from the pack," call the police for you if you give them a "code word, etc.)

Level four

Spread out Emergency resources or credit

Expecting your lowlife to keep cash immovably controlled, keeps the cash from you, or doesn't allow you to get your own money, will in general be trying to spread out an in-the-event account. Keep any change you can keep, return things to a store for cash back, hide any money given to you as a gift, or find substitute approaches to building some emergency cash. If you can't get emergency cash, make a pass at applying for a Mastercard in your name, yet be sure that you have declarations transported off a PO Box, a business district, or even to a buddy's home so your scoundrel doesn't find out. Make an effort not to get to your charge card account from your home PC.

Level Five

Make an escape plan

Pack and hide away a "get away from the sack." You should have an emergency sack with necessities in it. Be sure that you disguise the sack well in general (you could attempt to have to take off from it at someone else's home.) You pack light, but recall the going with for your sack

Changes of clothing for you and any adolescents

Copies of critical reports (birth confirmations, visas, driver's license, bank or Visa account information, etc)

www.ingramcontent.com/pod-product-compliance
Lightning Source LLC
LaVergne TN
LVHW080819170826
845678LV00011B/2076

* 9 7 9 8 3 5 9 4 8 2 8 6 8 *